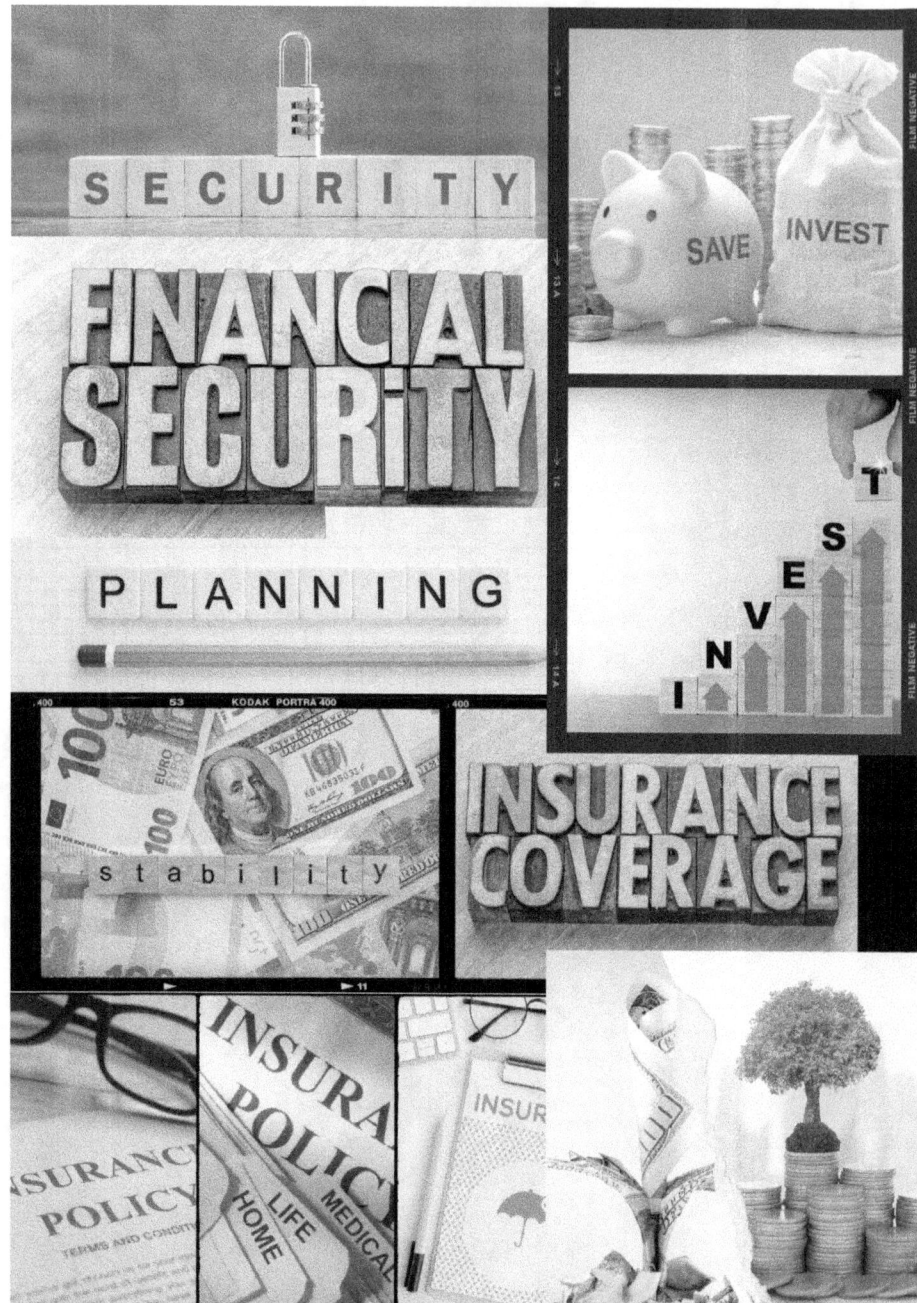

Securing Your Future: The Smart Guide to Life Insurance and Wealth Building

Table of Contents

Foreword – A Personal Note from the Author Severen Henderson

1. Understanding Life Insurance

(1) – The Purpose of Life Insurance

(2) – Key Terminology You Should Know

(3) – The Role of Life Insurance in Financial Planning

2. Assessing Your Insurance Needs

(1) – Evaluating Your Financial Responsibilities

(2) – Considering Current and Future Income Needs

(3) – How to Calculate Your Coverage Amount

3. Types of Life Insurance Policies

(1) – Term Life Insurance: Pros and Cons

(2) – Whole Life Insurance: A Comprehensive Look

(3) – Universal Life and Other Variants Explained

4. Life Insurance as a Wealth-Building Tool

(1) – Cash Value Accumulation Explained

(2) – Using Life Insurance for Retirement Income

(3) – Life Insurance as an Investment Vehicle

5. Tax Advantages of Life Insurance

(1) – Understanding Tax-Free Benefits

(2) - Tax Implications for Cash Value Growth

(3) - Using Life Insurance in Estate Planning

6. Customizing Your Policy

(1) - Riders: Add-Ons for Extra Protection

(2) - Choosing the Right Beneficiary Structure

(3) - Adjusting Coverage as Life Changes

7. Common Pitfalls in Life Insurance Purchases

(1) - Over-Insurance vs. Under-Insurance

(2) - Failing to Review Your Policy Regularly

(3) - Understanding Policy Exclusions and Limitations

8. Navigating the Policy Application Process

(1) - What to Expect During Underwriting

(2) - Essential Documents for Application

(3) - Tips for Getting Approved with Favorable Terms

9. Strategies for Maximizing Insurance Benefits

(1) - The Importance of Regular Policy Reviews

(2) - Leveraging Loans Against Cash Value

(3) - Making the Most of Dividends in Participating Policies

10. Case Studies: Real-Life Examples of Wealth Building

(1) - Young Families: Strategic Policy Use

(2) - Middle-Aged Professionals: Transitioning Wealth

(3) - Entrepreneurs: Life Insurance for Business Continuity

11. Life Insurance in Business Succession Planning

(1) - Key Person Insurance Explained

(2) - Buy-Sell Agreements and Life Insurance

(3) - Protecting Your Business Value Through Insurance

12. Adjusting Insurance for Life Changes

(1) - Impact of Marriage and Children on Coverage Needs

(2) - Changes in Employment and Their Influence

(3) - Planning for Retirement: Adjusting Your Strategy

13. The Future of Life Insurance

(1) - Trends Shaping the Insurance Industry

(2) - The Role of Technology in Policy Management

(3) - Emerging Products and New Market Opportunities

14. How to Choose Your Insurance Provider

(1) - Evaluating Financial Stability and Ratings

(2) - Importance of Customer Service and Reviews

(3) - Understanding Policy Terms and Carrier Options

15. Becoming a DIY Financial Planner

(1) - Resources for Self-Education on Insurance

(2) - Tools to Analyze and Compare Insurance Policies

(3) - Building a Comprehensive Financial Plan Including Insurance

Conclusion - Your Next Steps Toward a Secure and Prosperous Future

Foreword

A Personal Note from the Author

Dear Reader,

I know firsthand how overwhelming it can be when stepping into the world of life insurance and financial planning. Like many of you, I once viewed life insurance as something I had to have—an obligation rather than an opportunity. But as I dug deeper, I discovered something unexpected: life insurance wasn't just about protection; it was about empowerment, about creating options and peace of mind not just for me but also for my family and future generations.

Many online financial experts discuss various ways to make money and secure your financial future. However, sometimes, it feels like they are using complicated jargon and secrets to get you to spend money on projects that only benefit them. This book is different. My aim with it is to be straightforward and clear, explaining everything I've learned about financial security in easy-to-understand terms. After reading this book, I would love to connect with you to help you create a plan to achieve your financial goals.

When I first started learning about life insurance, I was trying to figure out how to ensure my loved ones would be okay if something happened to me. What I didn't realize was that I was unlocking a tool that could do so much more than that. After doing research and learning about it, I decided to get my life insurance license. I wanted to not only benefit from life insurance financially but also to help others achieve their goals in wealth building and financial security. Life insurance became more than just a safety net; it became a wealth-building strategy—a way to ensure my family could thrive and survive in the face of life's uncertainties.

This book is my way of sharing everything I've learned. It's not just a guide to policies and premiums; it's a roadmap to securing your financial future. Whether you're just starting and want to ensure your family is protected or you're looking for ways to leverage life insurance for long-term wealth building, there's something here for you.

I've sat across the table from families making tough decisions, listened to their fears, and helped them find the clarity they needed to take control of their financial lives. In every conversation, one thing was clear: when people are empowered with the right information, they can make incredible choices that improve their lives.

So, as you read this book, know that I'm not just giving you information—I'm sharing what has worked for me and countless others like you. I'm handing you a key to unlock not just protection but opportunity. I hope this book helps you see life insurance not as a burden or a mystery but as a tool you can wield to build the life you want for yourself and the people you love.

Let's embark on this journey together. Here's to your financial freedom, security, and peace of mind.

With gratitude and belief in your success,

Severen Henderson

1. Understanding Life Insurance

The Purpose of Life Insurance

Life insurance is a vital safety net for those who depend on you financially. When an unexpected death occurs, it can leave loved ones in a precarious position. The financial burden of daily living expenses, mortgage payments, education costs for children, and any debts can be overwhelming. Life insurance provides peace of mind, knowing that your family will have the financial security they need in a time of profound distress. This financial coverage can protect your dependents from the ripple effects of your untimely passing, allowing them to maintain their quality of life and focus on healing rather than financial worries.

Moreover, life insurance is a valuable buffer against unforeseen expenses that can arise at any moment. Medical emergencies, home repair costs, or other financial commitments do not pause during times of loss. A well-structured life insurance policy can address these unexpected financial challenges, allowing individuals and families to navigate through turbulent times without depleting savings or incurring crippling debt. It acts as a reassurance that, amidst the unpredictability of life, there is a plan to mitigate risks, ensuring that immediate and long-term financial needs can be met with less stress.

Understanding the layers of protection offered by life insurance can empower you to make informed choices that secure your family's future. Assessing your unique financial situation and the needs of your dependents is crucial. Be sure to explore the types of policies available and consider how each could affect your financial strategy. Strategically choosing life insurance prepares you for the unexpected and creates a foundation for your family's financial well-being.

Key Terminology You Should Know

Understanding premiums is crucial for anyone looking into life insurance. A premium is the amount you pay for your insurance policy, monthly, quarterly, or annually. This payment secures your coverage and can vary based on factors such as your age, health status, and the type of policy you choose. Higher premiums typically indicate broader coverage or benefits, while lower premiums might mean limited security. It's essential to find a balance between what you can afford and the level of coverage you need to ensure your loved ones are protected financially when you are no longer there.

When discussing beneficiaries, it's essential to clarify what this term means. A beneficiary is a person or entity you designate to receive the benefits from your policy when you pass away. This designation is significant because it ensures that the funds are directed to the individuals you trust most, thereby providing financial support to them in a difficult time. Naming a beneficiary can also help avoid complications and delays in probate proceedings. Reviewing your beneficiary choices periodically is wise since life changes, such as marriage, divorce, or childbirth, can impact your decisions. This will allow you to protect your family's interests and ensure your wishes are honored.

Understanding these key terms lays the foundation for effectively navigating the world of life insurance. As you think about your options, please remember to ask questions and seek clarity about premiums and beneficiaries. This knowledge will empower you to make thoughtful decisions that align with your financial goals and family's needs.

The Role of Life Insurance in Financial Planning

Life insurance is often seen merely as a safety net intended to protect loved ones in the event of an unexpected loss. However, it can play a crucial role in your overall financial planning. By incorporating life insurance into a comprehensive financial strategy, individuals can enhance their financial stability and support long-term growth. The right life insurance policy can provide immediate benefits through protection while also contributing to wealth accumulation over time. Many modern policies offer cash value components that can be accessed through loans or withdrawals, enabling policyholders to use those funds for significant life expenses such as education or a home purchase. This dual functionality transforms life insurance from a simple protective measure into a strategic financial asset that complements retirement plans and other investments.

Integrating this financial product within a well-structured plan can guide individuals toward their broader financial goals. It encourages disciplined savings, allowing policyholders to accumulate value and create a secure financial future. Moreover, life insurance proceeds can provide liquidity in financial emergencies, ensuring that loved ones are not burdened with debts or financial responsibilities in challenging times. The key to effectively leveraging life insurance lies in understanding where it fits within your financial picture and selecting the right policy that aligns with your personal goals.

Beyond immediate protection, life insurance offers powerful benefits for long-term financial security, particularly in achieving future financial goals like education and retirement. Many families prioritize saving for their children's education, and life insurance can be an invaluable tool in this regard. With specific policies, the cash value that builds over time can be borrowed against or withdrawn to cover education expenses. This means that instead of solely relying on traditional savings or investment accounts, parents can utilize life insurance to help bridge financial gaps when necessary, all while keeping their family's coverage intact.

To maximize these benefits, it is essential to assess individual insurance needs and select policies that best suit one's financial situation.

2. Assessing Your Insurance Needs

Evaluating Your Financial Responsibilities

Assessing your debts and expenses is a crucial first step in understanding your financial responsibility. It's important to take stock of all your current obligations, including credit card debts, loans, mortgages, and other bills. Once you know what you owe, you can better determine how much insurance coverage you need. This process not only helps in identifying immediate financial needs but also helps in estimating future expenses. Insurance should be viewed as a tool to protect your loved ones from potential financial burdens if the unexpected happens. Consider your current obligations; if something were to happen to you, how would your family manage? Evaluating your financial landscape will give you a clearer picture of your insurance needs and ensure your family's security.

Considering your future financial goals is equally important in shaping your insurance coverage requirements. Think about what you want to achieve—purchasing a home, funding your children's education, or planning for a comfortable retirement. Each goal may require different financial approaches, and your insurance plays a fundamental role in this planning. For instance, if you aim to build a higher net worth for retirement, specific life insurance policies can provide both coverage and an investment component, acting almost like a savings plan for the future. Balancing the desire for financial growth with the need for protection can create a cooperative strategy that ensures you work towards your goals while safeguarding your family should something happen. Always keep your life goals in perspective, as these aspirations will inform the amount and type of insurance coverage that suits your needs.

Understanding your current financial responsibilities and future goals can give you a strong foundation for making informed decisions about life insurance. As you evaluate what you owe and what you aspire to achieve, remember that life insurance isn't just about providing for the here and now. It is an integral part of a broader financial strategy that can lead to wealth-building over time. By thoughtfully assessing these areas, you can select insurance policies that protect your family's future and build long-term wealth, ensuring that you have both security and the ability to achieve your dreams.

Considering Current and Future Income Needs

Income replacement strategies are essential for ensuring your family can maintain their lifestyle during an unforeseen loss. Life insurance acts as a financial safety net, providing the necessary funds to cover daily expenses, mortgage payments, and future educational costs for children. Understanding how much coverage is needed involves assessing the total income your family relies on and estimating how long this income would need to be replaced. For many, factoring in debts, ongoing responsibilities, and possible future aspirations is crucial. Calculating these elements creates a solid foundation, aligning your insurance choices with your family's financial survival and overall well-being.

Adjusting for life changes requires a forward-thinking approach as household income can fluctuate significantly throughout careers. As your career progresses, salaries often increase, promotions become available, and additional income streams may emerge. It's vital to revisit your life insurance needs periodically, ideally whenever a significant life change, like a job change or the birth of a child. These events can lead to new financial responsibilities and aspirations, which may necessitate higher coverage amounts. Maintaining an adaptable insurance strategy helps ensure that your family is well-protected against potential risks while allowing for growth as your income and financial needs evolve.

Planning for both present and future income needs provides security and allows you to leverage life insurance as a strategic financial tool. Engaging in regular reviews of your policies makes sure they align with current life circumstances and future goals. This proactive approach can prevent underinsurance and position you to benefit from opportunities that arise as your career and life progress. Consider periodic consultations with a financial advisor to refine your insurance strategy, as their expertise can reveal how life insurance can serve not just as a safety net but as a powerful component of your broader wealth-building strategy.

How to Calculate Your Coverage Amount

The 10x Rule is a straightforward approach that many people find helpful when estimating their life insurance needs. Simply put, multiply your annual income by ten. If you earn $50,000 a year, you would consider a coverage amount of around $500,000. This estimate provides a basic starting point to ensure that your family's financial needs are met during your untimely passing. It considers factors such as paying off debts, covering daily living expenses, and planning for future major expenses like education for your children. While this method is not exhaustive, as it may overlook specific circumstances and other financial obligations, it simplifies the initial assessment process for those not deeply versed in insurance nuances.

As you delve deeper into your financial situation, consider additional variables beyond income. Consider existing savings, your spouse's income, children's financial needs, and other liabilities. The 10x Rule serves as a launching point that can be adjusted according to your unique situation. Still, it's wise to revisit this estimate periodically as your life situation changes, such as job promotions, increasing family sizes, or shifts in financial goals. Gathering these insights can provide a more tailored estimate of your insurance needs, leading to better financial security for your loved ones.

A detailed needs analysis can be incredibly useful for a more personalized approach to life insurance calculations. Numerous financial calculators available online help you dive deeper into your specific circumstances. These tools can account for various critical factors such as current debts, educational expenses for children, funeral costs, and the desired income replacement for your family. By inputting these details, the calculators can provide a tailored coverage amount that reflects your unique financial landscape.

3. Types of Life Insurance Policies

Term Life Insurance: Pros and Cons

Understanding the basics of term life insurance is essential for anyone exploring financial protection options. Term life insurance is a straightforward type of life insurance that provides coverage for a specific period, typically ranging from 10 to 30 years. Its primary purpose is to offer a death benefit to beneficiaries if the insured passes away during the term. This simplicity often translates to affordability, making term life popular among young professionals and families seeking financial security without breaking the bank. The lower premiums compared to whole-life policies allow individuals to obtain substantial coverage for a fraction of the cost, ensuring that loved ones are financially protected in case of an untimely death.

Choosing term life insurance can be particularly effective in various scenarios. For instance, young families experiencing the financial strain of raising children may find it ideal. Term life can cover the years until children are financially independent, ensuring that beneficiaries receive support during a critical time. Additionally, those with mortgages or other significant debts might opt for term life to guarantee that their family can maintain their lifestyle and meet financial obligations in their absence. It also suits individuals in stable career paths who anticipate enhanced earning potential in the future, as they can acquire the necessary coverage now while enjoying lower premiums. If plans change, terminating or converting the policy is often straightforward, making it a versatile option aligned with many life stages.

Understanding how term life insurance works allows individuals to evaluate their needs better. The goal is to ensure comprehensive coverage for dependents, perhaps during two decades when the financial impact of losing a contributor could be severe. Assessing personal circumstances, including debts, future obligations, and financial goals, informs decision-making. As you think about your financial future, remember that while term life insurance offers critical protection, it does not accumulate cash value, as whole life policies do. It's tempting to view insurance purely through the lens of protection, but considering its role in your broader financial strategy can maximize its benefits. Exploring options and adjusting as life evolves helps secure a more robust financial future.

Whole Life Insurance: A Comprehensive Look

Whole life insurance offers lifelong coverage, which means that as long as premiums are paid, the policy remains in force for your entire life. This level of security provides peace of mind, knowing that your loved ones will be protected financially no matter when you pass away. In contrast to term life insurance, which only covers you for a specified period, whole life expressly guarantees that your beneficiaries will receive a death benefit whenever you leave this world. This enduring security can ease anxiety about financial obligations and future uncertainties, especially for young and middle-aged adults who need assurance that their families will remain protected even if something unforeseen happens. The predictability of the policy also allows for better long-term financial planning, as you can include the assured death benefit into your estate strategy.

One of the standout features of whole life insurance is its ability to build cash value over time. This cash value grows at a guaranteed rate and may also earn dividends depending on the company's profitability. Over the years, the cash value can accumulate significantly, providing a financial asset that policyholders can tap into. Unlike the death benefit, paid out upon passing, the cash value can be accessed during your lifetime for various needs, such as funding a child's education, purchasing a home, or even supplementing retirement income. This dual benefit turns a policy into more than just a safety net; it becomes a versatile financial tool. However, it's essential to understand that accessing cash value may reduce the death benefit and that such withdrawals or loans typically come with interest charges. Thus, keeping a balanced view of how and when to access the cash value can greatly enhance your overall wealth strategy.

Universal Life and Other Variants Explained

Universal life insurance stands out because it offers the flexibility many individuals and families seek when planning their future. Unlike term life insurance, which provides coverage for a specific period, universal life policies allow policyholders to adjust their premiums and death benefits throughout their lives. If your financial situation changes—say you earn a promotion or face unexpected expenses—you can increase or decrease your premium payments accordingly. This adaptability helps you stay aligned with your financial goals while maintaining essential life insurance coverage.

Additionally, universal life policies have a cash value component that grows over time. This cash value is funded by the portion of your premium that goes beyond the cost of insurance and administrative expenses. Prevailing interest rates can influence the growth of this cash value, and it is accessible for loans or withdrawals when you need funds for emergencies or investments. However, it's crucial to remember that any money taken out will reduce the death benefit for your beneficiaries, so careful planning is necessary when utilizing these options.

In addition to traditional universal life insurance, other variants cater to different financial objectives and risk tolerances. Variable universal life insurance allows policyholders to invest the cash value in various investment options, such as stocks and bonds. This means the cash value can grow more rapidly than in standard universal policies, but it also comes with increased risks. If the market performs poorly, the cash value and possibly even the death benefit can decrease, making this option suitable for those more investment-savvy and comfortable with market fluctuations.

Indexed universal life insurance represents another innovative approach. It ties the growth of your cash value to a specific stock market index, such as the S&P 500. This means you can benefit from market gains without the full risk of market losses. Typically, these policies include a cap on the maximum return, which limits how much your cash value can grow in a good year. Understanding these intricate options is vital for those looking to blend insurance with savings and investment, offering a more robust approach to financial security.

When considering any of these life insurance options, evaluating your long-term goals, risk tolerance, and overall financial situation is essential. This thoughtful consideration can lead you to choose a policy that safeguards your family and contributes meaningfully to your wealth-building journey.

4. Life Insurance as a Wealth-Building Tool

Cash Value Accumulation Explained

The concept of cash value in life insurance revolves around certain policies that not only provide a death benefit but also accumulate cash over time. This cash value grows on a tax-deferred basis, meaning you won't owe taxes on this money as it increases. Whole life and universal life insurance policies are typically designed to build cash value. A portion of your premium payments goes towards this cash value, allowing it to grow steadily. It's important to understand that various factors like interest rates and the performance of the insurance company can influence this growth. This accumulation offers a unique financial advantage, effectively turning part of your life insurance into a savings component you can tap into when needed.

Using cash value effectively involves strategic planning to ensure you can access this money without jeopardizing your life insurance coverage. For instance, policyholders can take out loans against the cash value, which can be a flexible source of funds for emergencies, investments, or even life's unexpected turns. However, it's crucial to remember that any outstanding loans and interest will be deducted from the death benefit if not repaid. Alternatively, you can withdraw funds directly from the cash value, though this may reduce your death benefit and could have tax implications if you withdraw more than what you have paid into the policy. Understanding the terms and conditions tied to your specific policy can empower you to maximize your cash value while maintaining adequate coverage for your loved ones.

Regularly reviewing your policy and understanding how cash value works is key to maximizing its benefits. Staying informed about your policy's growth and options available for cash access can enhance your financial planning. Tapping into cash value should be part of a broader financial strategy, allowing you to leverage your insurance policy not just as protection but as a tool for building wealth. You can approach your insurance agent or financial advisor to explore how effectively using your policy's cash value can help you meet both short-term financial needs and long-term goals.

Using Life Insurance for Retirement Income

Life insurance is often viewed primarily as a safety net for your loved ones in the event of an untimely death, but it can be a valuable tool for enhancing your retirement income. Certain life insurance policies, like whole life and universal life, accumulate a cash value over time. This cash value can be tapped into during retirement, providing an additional income stream. The unique aspect of this strategy is that you can access your own money without needing to navigate traditional retirement accounts' limitations.

Imagine having a source of income that is reliable yet flexible, allowing you to maintain your lifestyle during retirement. As you pay premiums, some of that money builds up as cash value. You can take out loans against this cash value or withdraw funds, allowing you to use this money as needed. Some retirees find that they can effectively supplement their Social Security or pension payments using the cash value from their policies, giving them greater financial security and peace of mind.

One of the appealing features of using life insurance for retirement income is the potential for tax-free withdrawals. When you borrow against your policy's cash value, you do not incur taxes on the amount borrowed. You are taking a loan from your policy rather than withdrawing funds directly. The loan is not considered taxable income as long as the policy remains in force and does not lapse. However, it's essential to understand that unpaid loans will reduce the death benefit and the cash value, which could significantly impact your financial plans.

Understanding how to manage these loans and withdrawals is key to optimizing your retirement income strategy. It's advisable to monitor your policy regularly and consult a financial advisor to ensure you're on track to meet your retirement goals without jeopardizing your life insurance coverage. This awareness will help you balance utilizing your life insurance for retirement income while maintaining its intended purpose of providing a legacy for your loved ones.

Read the terms of your policy carefully. Each policy has different rules regarding withdrawals and loans, and knowing these upfront can save you from potential pitfalls. An informed approach will empower you to leverage your life insurance successfully as you navigate the complexities of retirement planning.

<u>Life Insurance as an Investment Vehicle</u>

Life insurance is often seen primarily as a safety net, a way to protect your loved ones in the event of an untimely passing. However, it can also be pivotal in a well-rounded investment portfolio. You are going beyond mere protection by including life insurance in your financial strategy. Some types of life insurance, particularly permanent policies like whole life or universal life insurance, accumulate cash value over time. This cash value can be accessed during your lifetime and can even serve as a source of funding for emergencies, significant purchases, or opportunities. Furthermore, life insurance may help diversify your investment portfolio, adding a layer of stability and predictability that traditional stock investments may not offer. Since the cash value grows on a tax-deferred basis, it acts as a unique savings vehicle, allowing you to build wealth while simultaneously gaining peace of mind knowing your family is protected.

Regarding investment strategies, it's essential to evaluate both the benefits and risks associated with using life insurance as a wealth-building tool. One significant advantage is the potential for tax-free loans against the cash value of a policy, which can be utilized for various financial needs without triggering immediate tax liabilities. In contrast, it's important to remain cautious, as life insurance policies can become complex and costly. High fees, surrender charges, and the potential for policy loans to erode death benefits are risks that need careful evaluation. Understanding these facets can guide you in choosing the right policy that aligns with your financial goals. It may be wise to work alongside a financial advisor who can help clarify these elements, ensuring you maximize your life insurance's protective and wealth-building aspects.

Before diving into a life insurance investment, consider your financial situation and long-term goals. Always do ample research and watch how different policies align with your unique needs. A practical tip is to regularly review your policy and consult with your financial planner to ensure that your chosen life insurance remains an integral part of your investment strategy, adapting as your financial landscape evolves.

5. Tax Advantages of Life Insurance

Understanding Tax-Free Benefits

Tax-free death benefits are one of the most compelling features of life insurance. When a policyholder passes away, the beneficiaries generally receive the death benefit free from federal income tax. This means that the full amount intended to provide financial support for loved ones, pay off debts, or fund future expenses is delivered without tax deductions. This tax advantage allows families to retain more of their inheritance, making life insurance an essential part of a comprehensive financial plan. However, the tax-free nature of these benefits comes with some important details that policyholders and beneficiaries should be aware of.

While the general rule is that life insurance payouts are tax-free, some exemptions and limitations can affect the tax status of these benefits. For example, if a policy is transferred to someone else and they become the policy's owner, the payout may not enjoy the same tax-free status due to cash value accumulation or possible federal gift tax implications. Additionally, suppose a policyholder takes out a loan against their life insurance policy. In that case, the outstanding loan amount will be deducted from the death benefit, which could create a taxable event if the remaining death benefit exceeds the cost basis. Understanding these nuances can help avoid surprises when the time comes to collect benefits, ensuring the family's financial future remains intact.

Tax Implications for Cash Value Growth

Cash value growth within certain life insurance policies is essential to understand, especially when considering its tax implications. The Internal Revenue Service (IRS) treats cash value growth as a unique financial component. As your cash value accumulates over time, it generally does so on a tax-deferred basis. This means that you don't pay taxes on the growth as it occurs, which can greatly enhance the accumulation potential of your policy. The tax-deferred status allows your money to grow faster than in a taxable account, where you would pay taxes on interest, dividends, and capital gains. One important point to note is that taxes are only due when you access this cash value, such as through a withdrawal or a loan against the policy, and even then, the tax implications can vary depending on how the withdrawal is structured.

Tax-deferred growth presents compelling advantages for long-term planning. Certain types of life insurance, such as whole life and universal life, allow individuals to accumulate cash value without immediate tax consequences. This feature can serve as an essential tool for wealth building. As your cash value grows, it can be used for various purposes, such as supplementing retirement income or funding major life expenses, allowing your investments to grow efficiently. It's also important to understand that if you pass away with an outstanding loan against your policy, your beneficiaries will receive the death benefit minus that loan amount. Therefore, awareness and strategic planning around cash value growth and its tax implications is crucial to maximizing the benefits for you and your family.

Consider reviewing your life insurance policy at regular intervals to effectively harness the benefits of tax-deferred cash value growth. As your financial situation changes, adjustments may be necessary to optimize growth. Additionally, working with a financial advisor who understands the specifics of tax laws and life insurance can provide valuable insights tailored to your circumstances. This proactive approach ensures that you are aware of the potential tax implications of accessing your cash value and leveraging them to bolster your financial objectives. Understanding these crucial aspects sets the groundwork for making informed decisions about your wealth-building strategy.

Using Life Insurance in Estate Planning

Life insurance can play a pivotal role in estate planning by providing the necessary financial support to loved ones when needed. By integrating a life insurance policy into your estate plan, you ensure that funds are available to cover immediate expenses, such as funeral costs, outstanding debts, and potential taxes on your estate. These funds can create a financial buffer, allowing beneficiaries to focus on grieving and adjusting to the loss without the pressure of financial burdens. Particularly when a family business or significant assets exist, life insurance can be set up to provide liquidity. This helps to ensure that your heirs do not have to liquidate investments or sell properties at an inopportune time, protecting the overall value of your estate. Structuring the policy effectively, perhaps as an irrevocable life insurance trust (ILIT), can further enhance its benefits by removing the death benefit from the taxable estate, thus maximizing what you pass on to your heirs.

When transferring wealth, life insurance can be one of the most tax-efficient tools available. By naming beneficiaries directly, you can pass on the death benefit without going through probate, which often delays access to funds and incurs additional costs. This means your loved ones can receive their inheritance quickly and without the tax implications that might accompany other forms of wealth transfer. Effective strategies such as gift exclusions for annual premiums can allow you to fund a policy while transferring wealth tax-free. By systematically gifting small amounts to cover premiums on a life insurance policy, you reduce your taxable estate while ensuring that your heirs are covered financially. It's also worth noting that when planned correctly, life insurance proceeds can be converted into cash over time through borrowings against the policy, allowing families to access funds without incurring taxes upfront, creating a dual benefit of protection and income.

Understanding the intricate relationship between life insurance and estate planning empowers you to make informed decisions that protect your family and secure your legacy. As you assess your financial situation, please consider seeking professional advice to tailor your insurance strategy to your unique needs, making sure that your wealth transfer plan is as effective and efficient as possible.

6. Customizing Your Policy

Riders: Add-Ons for Extra Protection

Riders are benefits attached to a life insurance policy that provides extra protection or enhance existing coverage. These add-ons cater to different financial needs and personal circumstances, making them essential to crafting the right policy for you. Common riders include the accelerated death benefit, which allows you to access part of your death benefit if you are diagnosed with a terminal illness, providing crucial funds during a challenging time. Another popular option is the waiver of premium rider, which ensures that your insurance remains in force even if you become disabled and can't pay the premiums. Child riders also offer coverage for your children at a low cost and can be converted into permanent policies later. Understanding these riders can help you customize your policy and ensure it truly suits your family's needs.

Selecting the right riders involves assessing your circumstances, goals, and challenges. You can start by thinking about what protections bring peace of mind to you and your family. A child rider might be a top priority if you have young children, ensuring they are covered under your policy. Also, please think about your health and potential future medical needs. If you have a family history of illness or you're concerned about the financial impact of severe health issues, an accelerated death benefit rider becomes invaluable. Evaluate your financial situation, too; if income loss due to temporary disability is a concern, including a waiver of premium could prevent you from losing your coverage. Ultimately, the best riders for you will align directly with your family's future needs and your long-term financial strategies. When reviewing options, don't hesitate to ask your insurance agent detailed questions about how each rider works and the costs involved.

As you navigate these choices, remember that flexibility is key. Life is unpredictable, and your insurance needs may change over time. Regularly reviewing your policy and its riders, especially during major life events like the birth of a child or changes in income, can ensure that your coverage remains relevant and sufficient. It's a proactive approach to safeguarding your family's financial future.

Choosing the Right Beneficiary Structure

Choosing the right beneficiary structure for your life insurance policy is crucial in ensuring your loved ones receive financial support when needed. The main types of beneficiaries include primary, secondary, and contingent beneficiaries. A primary beneficiary is the person or entity you designate to receive the death benefit directly upon your passing. This could be a spouse, child, or even a charity you support. Choosing someone you trust implicitly is essential, as this decision carries significant financial implications. Secondary beneficiaries, often called contingent beneficiaries, come into play if the primary beneficiary cannot claim the benefits for any reason, such as passing away before you do. Having a secondary beneficiary provides an additional layer of security and ensures that the funds will still be distributed according to your wishes. This layer can help avoid complications and delays in distributing your policy benefits, allowing your family to access funds quickly in a difficult time. Remember that if you name multiple primary beneficiaries, you also need to specify how the benefits should be split among them. Being clear about your intentions not only helps minimize confusion but also ensures that your financial legacy is honored in a way that reflects your wishes.

Naming a trust as a beneficiary of your life insurance policy can provide several advantages, especially for individuals with complex family dynamics or those wishing to manage how their assets are distributed after death. A trust can help avoid probate—an often lengthy and costly legal process for distributing assets—which is one of the most significant benefits of designating a trust as a beneficiary. When your policy names a trust as the beneficiary, the payout goes directly to the trust, allowing it to manage and distribute the funds according to your predefined plans without navigating the probate system. This can be particularly valuable for families with young children, as a trust can ensure the funds are used for their education and upbringing in a controlled manner. Furthermore, trusts can protect from creditors, ensuring that the benefits remain intact for your beneficiaries. However, it's essential to set up the trust correctly, with clear terms and an appointed trustee who understands your intentions. Mismanagement of the trust can lead to unintended consequences, so careful planning is key. Consulting with a financial advisor or an estate planning attorney is often wise to ensure that naming a trust as a beneficiary aligns with your overall financial goals and family needs.

Adjusting Coverage as Life Changes

Life is a series of milestones, each marking a significant shift that can affect your insurance needs. When you experience major events like getting married, having children, or buying a home, it's crucial to reassess your insurance policy. These life changes often bring new responsibilities and financial obligations, meaning your previous coverage may be inadequate. For instance, if you welcome a new child into your family, you may need to increase your life insurance to ensure they are financially secure in your absence. It's not just about having any coverage but having the right amount that aligns with your current situation. Regularly reviewing your policy ensures that it adapts to your life, providing the necessary protection for your loved ones as their needs evolve.

Financial changes also play a significant role in adjusting your coverage. As your income increases or decreases, or as your expenses shift due to factors like education costs or retirement planning, your insurance needs will likely change, too. It's essential to keep track of your financial situation and reflect that in your insurance coverage. For instance, a raise might encourage you to buy a larger policy to cover new debt, like a bigger mortgage or enhanced educational plans for your children. Alternatively, if you find yourself with rising expenses due to unexpected circumstances, maintaining the right level of coverage becomes crucial to safeguard against potential financial hardship. Being proactive about adjusting your life insurance can help ensure that you remain protected and prepared as your financial landscape changes.

Staying in tune with these life and financial changes isn't just about maintaining coverage; it's about leveraging your insurance as a strategic tool in your broader wealth-building plan. Regular adjustments allow you to maximize your policy's benefits and can potentially help you accumulate wealth over time. Knowing when to make these changes and having the foresight to act can significantly benefit your financial future. One practical tip is to set reminders to review your insurance coverage annually or following any major life event to ensure your policy aligns with your current needs and future goals.

7. Common Pitfalls in Life Insurance Purchases

Over-Insurance vs. Under-Insurance

Finding the right balance in insurance coverage is crucial for financial security. Too much insurance, known as over-insurance, can lead to excessive premiums that strain your budget without providing substantial additional benefits. Conversely, under-insurance leaves you vulnerable to significant risks and potentially devastating financial consequences. It's essential to evaluate your unique circumstances, including your family's needs, outstanding debts, and future goals, to ascertain the appropriate level of coverage. Understand that the ideal policy should give you peace of mind without causing unnecessary financial burdens.

Tailoring your insurance policy involves a careful assessment of your situation. Consider your age, health status, occupation, and financial responsibilities when customizing your coverage. Engaging with a knowledgeable insurance agent can be invaluable. They possess the expertise to guide you through various options, helping to establish a policy that aligns with your lifestyle and long-term aspirations. Make use of tools like life insurance calculators to estimate your necessary coverage amount, ensuring you have enough to protect your loved ones while finding ways to integrate the policy into your broader financial strategy. This thoughtful approach will secure your family's future and pave the way toward building lasting wealth.

In your quest to find the right insurance balance, frequently reassess your needs as circumstances change. Life events like marriage, home purchases, or the birth of a child may require you to adjust your coverage to remain adequately protected. Keeping your insurance updated is a practical way to ensure you have the right safety nets while optimizing your financial resources.

Failing to Review Your Policy Regularly

Reviewing your insurance policy regularly is essential for ensuring it aligns with your current life circumstances and financial goals. Life is constantly changing—new jobs, growing families, changing health conditions, and evolving financial situations. These changes can impact the adequacy of your coverage. If you neglect to review your policy, you risk being underinsured or overpaying for coverage you no longer need. Regular reviews can uncover gaps in your protection or opportunities to optimize your benefits.

Understanding the full scope of your insurance means you can confidently make informed decisions tailored to your needs.

Several signs indicate that it's time to take a closer look at your insurance policy. A significant life event, such as the birth of a child, marriage, or purchasing a new home, prompts a review to ensure your coverage meets the latest demands on your finances. Additionally, changes in your income or unexpected medical issues should signal a policy reassessment. If your lifestyle has shifted significantly—like starting a business or nearing retirement—you might need different types of coverage or higher limits. Recognizing these indicators early allows you to address potential deficiencies, ensuring your insurance serves its purpose effectively.

A practical tip is to schedule a regular review of your insurance policy, perhaps annually or after major life changes. Having a set time in your calendar helps make policy reviews a habit, ensuring you're always aware of your coverage. This proactive approach will lead to better financial security and peace of mind as you adapt to life's changes and complexities.

Understanding Policy Exclusions and Limitations

Recognizing the fine print is crucial in understanding your insurance policy. Many policyholders overlook exclusions and limitations, which can leave them feeling frustrated when a claim is denied. These exclusions refer to the specific situations or circumstances under which your insurance policy will not provide coverage. For instance, if your policy excludes coverage for certain pre-existing health conditions, it is important to recognize that this could impact your claims significantly. Understanding the exclusions can help you make informed decisions when selecting policies that align with your risk profile and financial goals. It can also clarify what is at stake if something unexpected happens.

Common exclusions may vary between different insurance providers and policy types. A typical example is the exclusion of coverage for acts of war or natural disasters, which can be surprising for some policyholders. Other common exclusions might include suicide in the first two years of the policy or non-disclosure of crucial information during the application process. Recognizing these exclusions can help you avoid potential pitfalls when it comes time to file a claim. Also, understanding the typical limitations that might apply, such as caps on payouts or specific waiting periods, can help you in formulating a comprehensive financial strategy to maximize the benefits of your policy.

Be proactive in reviewing your policy's terms. It can be beneficial to discuss with your insurance agent to clarify any exclusions and limitations that are not immediately clear. Being well-informed means you can tailor your insurance selection process to better match your needs, reducing the likelihood of unwelcome surprises when claiming benefits. Moreover, remember this understanding as part of your broader financial planning strategy, as this knowledge allows you to integrate life insurance effectively into your long-term wealth-building goals.

8. Navigating the Policy Application Process

What to Expect During Underwriting

Underwriting is crucial in the insurance application process as it helps insurers assess the risk of insuring an applicant. Underwriting determines whether an applicant is eligible for coverage and what premium they should pay based on their risk profile. The underwriter evaluates factors such as the applicant's health, lifestyle, and family medical history. This evaluation ensures that the insurer can balance the risk of potential payouts with the premiums collected, making underwriting an essential step in establishing the terms of a life insurance policy. By analyzing information provided in the application and possibly requesting additional medical records or tests, underwriters ensure that they assign appropriate conditions to each policy.

Your health and lifestyle significantly impact underwriting outcomes. Underwriters look closely at medical history, chronic conditions, and past surgeries or treatments when determining eligibility. If an applicant has health issues like diabetes or heart disease, they may face higher premiums or even denial of coverage. Lifestyle choices also play a role; for example, smokers typically pay more than non-smokers because they present a higher risk for health issues. Other factors include occupation and hobbies. Dangerous jobs or risky activities can increase your premium or make securing coverage difficult. Understanding these influences helps potential policyholders prepare and take steps to improve their risk profile before applying for life insurance.

Applicants need to be honest and thorough when filling out their insurance applications. Discrepancies or omissions can result in delayed coverage or denied claims in the future. Preparing for underwriting by reviewing your health status and considering your lifestyle can significantly impact the overall experience. Additionally, if you have concerns about specific factors affecting your underwriting, consider discussing them with an insurance agent. They can guide how to present your application best, potentially leading to a more favorable assessment.

Essential Documents for Application

To complete your application for life insurance, you will need various important documents. These documents help insurance companies gauge your risk profile and ensure that you receive appropriate coverage. First, personal identification is essential. This can be a government-issued photo ID, such as a driver's license or passport, which verifies your identity. Additionally, you will be asked for proof of income. This typically includes recent pay stubs, W-2 forms, or bank statements that reflect your earning history. Your social security number is another crucial information that may be required for verification. If you're married or have dependents, documentation such as marriage or birth certificates for your children will also be necessary. These documents confirm your familial relationships and assist in determining coverage amounts based on your responsibilities.

As you prepare for the application process, it's wise to anticipate common questions that may arise. Insurance agents often inquire about your health history. This includes any pre-existing conditions, medications you currently take, and any significant surgeries you may have undergone. Understanding this aspect of your health is vital as it affects your policy premiums and coverage eligibility. You can also expect questions about your lifestyle choices, such as smoking habits or engagement in high-risk activities like extreme sports. These factors significantly influence the terms of your policy.

Furthermore, be prepared to discuss your financial goals and your reasons for seeking life insurance. Clarity about how much coverage you want and why will help agents tailor options that best fit your needs. Having answers to these questions ready will streamline the process and lead to a more accurate assessment of your insurance needs.

Gathering these essential documents and preparing for potential questions facilitates a smoother application process and empowers you to make informed decisions about your life insurance needs. As a practical tip, consider scheduling a time to review your documents with an insurance professional, ensuring everything is in order before you start the application process.

Tips for Getting Approved with Favorable Terms

Improving your chances of getting approved for life insurance with favorable terms requires a strategic approach. You can start by understanding your financial situation, including your income, expenses, and debts. This comprehensive understanding lays the groundwork for presenting yourself as a lower-risk candidate to insurance companies. Additionally, maintaining a good credit score can significantly enhance approval odds. Insurers often check your credit history, and a higher score indicates reliability. Consider reducing high credit card balances and ensuring all bills are paid on time. When applying for insurance, providing accurate and honest information is also helpful. Any discrepancies could lead to higher premiums or even denial of coverage. Moreover, don't hesitate to consult with a financial advisor to assess your insurance needs thoroughly and incorporate them into your broader financial strategy.

Working with a knowledgeable agent can be a game changer in securing favorable terms for your life insurance. A skilled agent understands the nuances of various policies and can also navigate the complexities of different insurers' requirements. They can help you find the best fit for your unique situation, factoring in your budget, health, and family needs. An agent can explain the intricacies of policy features, such as riders that offer additional benefits or options to access cash value in certain policies. Having someone on your side who is experienced in the industry can provide peace of mind, as they'll handle most of the legwork, allowing you to focus on your family's financial future. Furthermore, a seasoned agent may have insights on leveraging specific policies as wealth-building tools, helping you secure protection and a path toward long-term financial growth.

9. Strategies for Maximizing Insurance Benefits

The Importance of Regular Policy Reviews

Establishing a regular review schedule for your life insurance policy is essential for ensuring that your coverage meets your evolving needs. Best practices suggest that you should plan to review your policy at least once a year. This annual review allows you to assess your coverage in light of changes in your financial status, family circumstances, or overall health. Consider setting a specific date, such as your policy anniversary or a significant date like your birthday, to remind yourself to conduct this important review. In addition, align your reviews with other financial planning activities, such as tax preparation or budget reviews, to create a comprehensive financial overview.

During each review, focus on whether your coverage adequately supports your family's financial goals. Evaluate your coverage amounts and whether your beneficiaries are up to date. Major lifestyle events—like a new job, a home purchase, or the birth of a child—can significantly change your insurance needs. Furthermore, if you've acquired new assets or your financial situation has improved, you may want to consider increasing your coverage. Keeping a log of your review findings helps track changes over the years and simplifies understanding how your needs have evolved.

Life is full of changes, and each transition can require adjustments to your insurance policy. For instance, if you welcome a new child into your family, it's crucial to re-evaluate your life insurance coverage. The financial needs of a new family member can substantially increase your responsibilities, and your policy should reflect that. Likewise, significant changes in your marital status, such as marriage or divorce, should trigger a review of beneficiaries and coverage amounts. This is also true when you buy a home or take on debt; increased financial obligations require higher coverage or specific protections.

In addition to these major life events, maintaining an awareness of your health changes is equally important. If you experience a significant change in your health status, you may find that certain types of insurance become more expensive or even unavailable to you. So, addressing these aspects proactively makes sure you maintain the best coverage. Regular communication with your insurance agent can also facilitate swift adjustments. They can offer advice tailored to your unique circumstances, helping you navigate the complexities of policy modifications while ensuring your financial future remains secure.

Remember that life insurance isn't a one-time decision; it's an ongoing part of your financial strategy that adapts as your life evolves. Taking proactive steps ensures that your insurance remains a functional tool in preserving your family's financial security and long-term wealth.

Leveraging Loans Against Cash Value

Life insurance policies accumulate cash value over time, particularly whole and universal life insurance. This cash value can be accessed through a policy loan, allowing policyholders to borrow against it without undergoing a credit check or lengthy approval process. When you take out a loan against your policy's cash value, you're borrowing your own money, which means there are no restrictions on how you can use those funds. Understanding the mechanics of policy loans is crucial. The amount you can borrow is generally determined by the accumulated cash value in your policy, and the loans are typically charged an interest rate. This interest can vary depending on your policy type, so reviewing your policy documents is advisable for clarity.

One appealing aspect of policy loans is that they do not require regular repayment schedules like traditional ones. However, it is essential to remember that any unpaid loan balance and interest will be subtracted from the death benefit your beneficiaries receive when you pass away. If the loan amount plus interest exceeds your policy's cash value, it could lead to a lapse in your policy. Always understand the implications for your policy's health and financial future before deciding to borrow against it.

While accessing funds through a policy loan can be beneficial, using such loans responsibly is key to maintaining your financial health. Establishing a clear purpose for the loan can help guide your decision-making process. For example, consider using borrowed funds to invest in opportunities that may yield a higher return than the interest rate on your loan. This could include funding a business venture, homing in on educational pursuits, or managing unexpected expenses. The idea is to leverage the benefits of the loan effectively, ensuring that the policy loan aids your overall financial strategy.

Repaying your policy loans is equally important. Although repayment is flexible, proactively making payments can help minimize the accrual of interest and preserve the integrity of your life insurance policy. If possible, consider setting up a repayment plan that aligns with your cash flow to ensure that your loan does not negatively impact your policy in the long term. Setting reminders and treating these repayments with the same seriousness as other financial obligations can keep your policy active and your financial goals on track.

Remember, the power of compound interest works both ways: while it can enhance your savings, it can also increase the amount you owe. Being mindful of this dynamic can help you leverage the advantages of a policy loan while guarding against potential pitfalls that might arise from mismanagement.

Making the Most of Dividends in Participating Policies

Dividends in participating whole life insurance policies are a unique feature that allows policyholders to benefit from the company's financial performance. Unlike traditional whole-life policies that do not pay dividends, participating policies share the company's surplus profits with their policyholders. This means that when the insurance company does well, you potentially reap the rewards. These dividends can be viewed as a return on the safety net you provide, contributing to your financial security. It's important to recognize that while these dividends are not guaranteed, they are a regular feature of many mutual insurance companies, which tend to have a strong history of paying dividends.

Understanding how dividends work involves knowing how they are calculated. Insurance companies typically base their dividends on factors such as investment performance, mortality rates, and administrative costs. Policyholders receive annual statements detailing the dividend declarations, which can be used in various beneficial ways. Many see dividends as an opportunity to reduce premiums, increase the policy's cash value, or even receive them as cash payments. Each option can help enhance your wealth-building strategy while providing considerable flexibility in managing your policy over time.

Utilizing dividends effectively allows policyholders to enhance their financial strategy significantly. One popular option is to use dividends to purchase additional paid-up insurance. This effectively increases your death benefit without submitting additional applications or undergoing medical examinations. It not only boosts your protection but also enhances the cash value accumulation of your policy, providing you with a more substantial asset down the line.

Another strategic use of dividends is opting for them in cash. This provides immediate liquidity that you can use for immediate needs or investments outside your policy. However, it's essential to recognize that while taking dividends in cash offers flexibility, it could also slow down the overall growth of your policy's cash value over time. Some policyholders may also choose to reinvest dividends back into the policy, adding to the cash value and potentially compounding their growth significantly. This approach can be particularly powerful over the long term.

I think it's a good idea to consult with a financial advisor to discuss which dividend strategy aligns with your long-term financial goals and situation. Remember, the goal is not just to accumulate wealth but to do so in a way that provides maximum benefit and security for you and your loved ones.

10. Case Studies: Real-Life Examples of Wealth Building

Young Families: Strategic Policy Use

One young family discovered the power of life insurance early in their journey of parenthood. Shortly after the birth of their first child, they realized the importance of securing their family's financial future. They decided to purchase a term life insurance policy covering their mortgage and ensuring their child's education. This decision provided them with immediate peace of mind, knowing that their loved ones would be financially protected if the unexpected occurred. Over time, they also explored permanent life insurance options that combined protection with a cash value that could grow over the years. This has given them long-term benefits, allowing them to tap into that cash value for emergencies or future investments while maintaining coverage for their family. With thoughtful planning, this family secured immediate needs and laid a solid foundation for their financial future, demonstrating how strategic life insurance can benefit young families.

From their experiences, other families have gathered several lessons. One important takeaway is that life insurance should not be viewed simply as an expense but rather as a crucial investment in their family's security and future. Understanding individual needs is vital, as each family has unique circumstances that should guide policy choices. Many families also learned the importance of regular policy reviews to adjust coverage according to life changes, such as having more children or changes in income. Educating themselves about different policy types—like term and whole life—helped them make informed choices aligned with their financial goals. This ongoing education also highlighted the potential of life insurance as a powerful financial tool, not just a safety net. By sharing these insights and encouraging open conversations about financial planning, families can better prepare themselves for the future, ensuring that life insurance serves its purpose effectively.

Families looking to maximize their life insurance benefits should consider starting discussions about coverage early in their journey and maintaining an open dialogue about evolving financial needs.

Middle-Aged Professionals: Transitioning Wealth

Many middle-aged professionals encounter pivotal moments that shift their financial landscape, often requiring a deft approach to wealth management. Insurance can play a critical role during these transitions. For instance, consider the story of Maria, a 45-year-old corporate executive who recently inherited a substantial sum from her parents. Instead of simply adding to her investment portfolio, Maria explored how her existing life insurance policy might assist in immediate financial security and long-term wealth creation. By converting her term policy to a whole-life policy, she could retain protection while also creating a cash value that could supplement her retirement savings. This strategic pivot not only safeguarded her family's future but also positioned her to invest wisely for the years to come.

Another compelling example comes from Tom, a 50-year-old entrepreneur faced with a sudden business downturn due to unexpected market changes. Tom turned to his whole life insurance policy to stabilize his financial situation. He took out a policy loan against his built cash value over the years. This option provided immediate liquidity without triggering a taxable event, allowing him to weather his business challenges. By leveraging his insurance intelligently, Tom could cover crucial expenses and explore new business avenues without the constant strain of financial anxiety. These narratives reflect how the right insurance strategies can cushion individuals during transitions and pave the way for future growth.

Adjusting insurance policies over time is a natural and necessary part of financial planning for middle-aged professionals. As life circumstances evolve, so too should one's coverage. Emily, a 48-year-old mother of three, realized her needs changed drastically when her children reached college age. Initially, she had a significant amount of term life insurance to protect her family during their younger years. With reduced financial responsibilities, she decided to convert part of her term policy to a universal life policy. This decision allowed her to reduce premiums on the term coverage while starting to accumulate cash values that could be accessed later for her children's education expenses or her retirement savings.

Similarly, David, nearing retirement, found that his needs had also shifted. After payroll cuts at his company, he was concerned about his anticipated retirement income. With the cash value of his existing life insurance policy, David explored options to adjust coverage and convert some of his insurance into an annuity. This not only provided a steady income but also maintained a death benefit for his spouse, securing their financial future. These instances highlight the importance of regularly reviewing and adjusting insurance policies to align with changing life events, ensuring that the financial strategies remain effective and relevant.

Understanding how to navigate these adjustments is vital for anyone looking to transition wealth effectively. Regular policy reviews, open discussions with insurance professionals, and a proactive approach to financial planning can empower individuals to maximize their insurance benefits while adapting to life's changing dynamics.

Entrepreneurs: Life Insurance for Business Continuity

Entrepreneurs often put in countless hours and significant financial resources to build their businesses, making protecting that value through smart strategies essential. Life insurance has proven to be a crucial tool for many successful business owners looking to secure their companies' futures. Take, for example, the story of a small business owner in the tech industry who unexpectedly passed away. With a robust life insurance policy, his family could pay off the business debts and maintain ownership in the company instead of forcing a sale or liquidation. This insurance preserved the business value and allowed the surviving family members to keep the entrepreneurial dream alive.

Similarly, another entrepreneur in the restaurant industry secured a policy that funded a buy-sell agreement with a business partner. When he passed away prematurely, the insurance provided the funds needed for the partner to buy out his share, ensuring the restaurant continued operating without disruption. These real-life examples illustrate how strategically implemented life insurance can protect a business's legacy, providing peace of mind to entrepreneurs and their families.

A well-thought-out business succession plan that includes life insurance is vital for entrepreneurs. Such plans ensure that a business can continue seamlessly during an unexpected loss. When entrepreneurs take time to assess their business structure and plans, they can integrate suitable life insurance products tailored to their unique situations. For instance, if an entrepreneur has family members involved in the business, placing them as beneficiaries on a life insurance policy can provide them with immediate funds necessary for transitioning leadership or managing ongoing expenses. This foresight supports business continuity and reassures employees and customers that the company will endure. Moreover, a solid succession plan, including insurance, can help to avoid conflict among stakeholders during challenging times. By making clear arrangements now, entrepreneurs can ensure their hard work remains intact, and their vision continues, paving the way for future generations to thrive.

Understanding these concepts is vital; entrepreneurs should view life insurance as an expense and an investment into their businesses and their family's future. Evaluating different life insurance options and integrating them into a comprehensive business plan can safeguard against unforeseen events, ensuring that the businesses they've built can continue to prosper regardless of life's unpredictability. As a practical tip, entrepreneurs should regularly review their insurance policies and succession plans to align with their evolving business goals and personal circumstances, ensuring their protections remain robust and relevant.

11. Life Insurance in Business Succession Planning

Key Person Insurance Explained

Key Person Insurance is a specific type of life insurance designed to protect a business from financial loss that may occur when a vital member of the organization passes away or becomes unable to work. This individual, often a founder, owner, or high-level executive, is integral to the company's success. Their unique skills, relationships, and knowledge can be critical assets, and losing them can create significant disruption. Understanding the importance of insuring these key people is crucial for any business owner or entrepreneur. It helps ensure that the company can sustain its operations during a challenging transition and provides the necessary capital to implement succession plans, covering the loss of revenue and providing a buffer against unforeseen circumstances. Essentially, this type of insurance is not just about protecting the business financially but also about maintaining stability and confidence among clients, employees, and investors during difficult times.

The benefits of Key Person Coverage extend beyond mere financial reimbursement. This insurance allows businesses to cover the costs of hiring a replacement, integrating new talent, or even temporarily filling the gap during the transition. It can also ease the minds of investors and stakeholders, demonstrating that the organization is prepared for the unexpected and has strategies to safeguard its future. Additionally, having this coverage means that a business will have immediate funds readily available to navigate through a critical period without jeopardizing its ongoing operations. Companies equipped with Key Person Insurance can quickly initiate recovery plans and reassess business strategies with a clearer financial shield against the potential chaos of losing a pivotal team member. Ultimately, this type of insurance protects the bottom line and serves as a testament to a well-rounded, proactive approach to business sustainability. It highlights the foresight of business leaders in securing their legacy and operations in the face of uncertainty.

One practical step for business owners is to thoroughly evaluate their key personnel. Identifying who the key people are and understanding their roles within the organization can create a clearer picture of what coverage might be necessary. This means looking at who generates revenue or leads teams and considering individuals whose expertise and decision-making ability drive the company's vision forward. Once that is established, seeking professional advice to determine the right amount of coverage can significantly help in tailoring an effective Key Person Insurance policy that meets the business's unique needs.

Buy-Sell Agreements and Life Insurance

A buy-sell agreement is a vital document for business continuity. It outlines what happens to a business if one of the owners can no longer participate, whether due to death, disability, or another unforeseen circumstance. This agreement provides a clear plan for transferring ownership and minimizes conflict among surviving partners or family members. A buy-sell agreement ensures that the business can continue to operate smoothly by preventing complications such as disputes over ownership shares or valuation discrepancies. By establishing predetermined terms, all parties can confidently navigate the challenging times following an owner's departure, allowing the remaining partners or heirs to focus on the business rather than get caught in a tangled legal process.

Integrating life insurance into buy-sell agreements can significantly enhance the funding mechanism for these agreements. The surviving business owners typically purchase life insurance policies on each other's lives, which serve as a financial safety net when an owner's death occurs. Upon the death of one partner, the life insurance payout provides the funds necessary to buy out the deceased owner's share, making it easier for the surviving partners to maintain control of the business without struggling to raise capital. This protects the business and ensures that the deceased owner's family receives fair compensation, honoring their loved one's contribution while securing the future of the business. As you plan your buy-sell agreement, considering life insurance as a funding option can provide peace of mind and a more stable financial pathway for all parties involved.

When crafting a buy-sell agreement funded by life insurance, reviewing the policies and addressing any changes in ownership shares over time is crucial. Regular check-ins can ensure that the coverage remains adequate as the business evolves and that the agreements reflect current valuations. Engaging a legal expert or financial advisor can be beneficial in drafting and updating these agreements to keep them relevant and effective. By proactively addressing these aspects, business owners can safeguard their interests and build a resilient framework supporting their enterprise and their families.

Protecting Your Business Value Through Insurance

Every business has a value that goes beyond its tangible assets like real estate and equipment. Understanding this value is essential for securing the future of your business, especially when it comes to insurance. To assess your business value accurately, start by evaluating key components such as your revenue streams, customer base, brand reputation, and market position. This will help you arrive at a realistic valuation. Consider hiring a professional appraiser specializing in identifying and quantifying a business's worth. They can provide an objective analysis that could reveal insights you may not have considered. The valuation process should not be a one-time event; regular assessments are crucial to keep track of growth and changing market conditions. This continual process allows you to adapt your business strategies effectively and ensures that your insurance coverage aligns with its current worth.

Implementing the right insurance strategies can be a game changer in preserving the value of your business. Start with foundational insurance types such as general liability, property, and business interruption insurance. These cover essential risks and help you recover quickly from unforeseen events. Additionally, consider professional liability insurance if your business provides services, as this protects against claims of negligence or malpractice. Beyond the basics, utilize key-person insurance to cover potential losses caused by the unexpected absence of essential personnel. This type of insurance ensures that your operations can continue smoothly even in challenging situations, safeguarding its overall value. Another smart strategy is to invest in business owner's policies that bundle multiple types of coverage at a discounted rate, providing more comprehensive protection at a lower cost. Don't overlook the value of regular insurance coverage reviews as your business evolves. This proactive approach ensures you are never underinsured and keeps your business well-prepared to face any challenges. Prioritizing these strategies will help maintain and possibly enhance the value of your business, allowing it to thrive even amidst uncertainties.

12. Adjusting Insurance for Life Changes

Impact of Marriage and Children on Coverage Needs

Reassessing your insurance needs after getting married and having children is crucial for ensuring your family's financial security. A marriage often leads to shared finances and combined responsibilities, which means your insurance policies may need to reflect this new reality. You can start by evaluating your current coverage to see if it aligns with your new lifestyle. Factors such as dual incomes, joint debts, and shared expenses should all be considered. Consider how much coverage is needed to replace lost income in case of an unforeseen event, ensuring your partner can maintain their standard of living.

Additionally, when children enter the picture, they are responsible for providing for their future well-being. This means factoring in costs like education, childcare, and everyday expenses. Adjusting your life insurance policy can help create a safety net that keeps your loved ones secure, especially during the formative years of your children's lives.

Planning for growing families involves assessing current needs and anticipating future changes. As your family expands, so do your financial responsibilities. It's important to consider how many dependents you may have in the coming years. Many policies allow for adjustments as your situation evolves, so look for flexible options. You might want policies that cover not just your current children but also any future kids or even extended family members who might depend on you.

Moreover, establishing a policy that can grow with your family can provide peace of mind. Consider the potential addition of college funds or increased healthcare costs as children age. By proactively preparing your policies now, you'll avoid scrambling later when life gets busier. Reviewing and adjusting your life insurance in the context of growing dependents can be a significant step toward securing your family's financial future.

Changes in Employment and Their Influence

Changes in employment status can significantly impact your life insurance situation. When you switch jobs or face a change in your employment status, it often leads to a reevaluation of your life insurance coverage. Many people rely on employer-provided life insurance, which can be beneficial because it often comes at little or no cost. However, this coverage may no longer be in effect once you change jobs. It's critical to assess your life insurance needs during these transitions. Your coverage may have protected your family in the event of unforeseen circumstances. If that policy disappears, securing an alternative to ensure your loved ones remain protected is essential. Thinking proactively about life insurance can help you avoid financial repercussions caused by employment changes.

Additionally, understanding your rights regarding group life insurance can offer peace of mind. For instance, you may have the option to convert your group policy into an individual policy, allowing you to maintain some level of coverage. Consider speaking with an insurance advisor to explore the best options for transferring or supplementing your coverage in light of these job changes. Remember, the value of life insurance lies in its ability to provide security and ensure that your loved ones' financial needs are met no matter where your career takes you.

Evaluating employer-provided insurance options is vital as they can vary greatly regarding benefits and limitations. Group insurance offers lower premiums than individual policies since the risk is spread across a larger pool of employees. However, this coverage may only sometimes be sufficient for your family's long-term needs. It's crucial to thoroughly review the specifics of your employer's plan, such as the amount of coverage offered, the process for filing claims, and whether the policy includes additional benefits like accidental death coverage or disability clauses.

Just to let you know, using group life insurance can be risky. If you leave your job, you might lose that coverage or undergo a complicated conversion process. Weighing the benefits and limitations of group insurance against individual policies is a critical step in financial planning. As you assess these options, consider factors such as your current financial responsibilities, future goals, and how much coverage your family will need to maintain their living standards if something happens to you. A thorough understanding of your insurance options will help you make informed decisions that align with your overall financial strategy, ensuring you build a secure and resilient future for yourself and your loved ones.

Revisiting your insurance needs whenever your employment status changes is a good practice. This allows you to stay ahead and always provide for your family.

Planning for Retirement: Adjusting Your Strategy

As you approach retirement, you must reassess your life insurance needs. During your working years, life insurance often serves as a safety net for your family, ensuring that debts are paid off and that your loved ones maintain their lifestyle in your absence.

However, when retirement nears, the significance of that protection can shift. Many people find they no longer have the same financial obligations, such as a mortgage or dependent children's education costs. This shift may lead to reconsidering how much life insurance coverage is necessary. It's important to understand that while some needs may decrease, others may arise, such as final expenses, taxes, or leaving a legacy for heirs. Additionally, your need for life insurance as a wealth-building tool could become more pronounced if you have investment accounts, retirement funds, or other assets. The right coverage can help ensure that these assets are preserved for your family and not diminished by taxes or other costs upon your passing.

Transitioning your life insurance policy as you approach retirement involves carefully evaluating your current policy and aligning it with your future needs. For many, this can mean converting a term policy into a permanent one, providing additional benefits like cash value accumulation. Cash value life insurance offers a way to build wealth while still providing a death benefit, allowing you to tap into the policy's value in retirement if necessary. It's crucial to review your policy's terms, fees, and growth potential when considering this shift. Communicating with an insurance agent can help illuminate options you might not be aware of, including riders that can enhance your coverage. For example, long-term care riders provide support if you require assistance with daily living activities. Moreover, be mindful of timing; making changes too close to retirement can lead to unexpected costs or coverage gaps. Instead, plan well in advance to ensure that your life insurance aligns seamlessly with your overall financial strategy as you transition into this new life phase.

When evaluating how much insurance you'll still need after retirement, consider consulting a financial advisor to help clarify your total financial picture, including assets, liabilities, and any income sources you might have during retirement. This holistic view will guide you in making informed decisions about your life insurance policy adjustments.

13. The Future of Life Insurance

Trends Shaping the Insurance Industry

Emerging trends reshape the insurance landscape, influencing how policies are structured and bought. Digital transformation is a key driver, enabling insurers to streamline processes and enhance customer experience. Customers increasingly expect personalized services and instant access to information, pushing companies toward digital platforms that provide real-time quotes and policy management. Artificial intelligence and machine learning allow insurers to analyze data more effectively, leading to better risk assessment and more tailored products. At the same time, sustainability is gaining traction as a concern for consumers; they prefer insurers that demonstrate social responsibility and eco-consciousness. This shift prompts insurers to develop green policies and engage in practices that reduce environmental impact while providing coverage. The focus on health and wellness is also emerging, with companies encouraging healthier lifestyles among policyholders by offering incentives such as lower premiums for maintaining a healthy lifestyle or participating in wellness programs. These trends indicate a move toward a more responsive, customer-centric insurance industry that prioritizes technology, sustainability, and health.

Consumer preferences are evolving rapidly, reflecting broader changes in society. Today's consumers are more informed and empowered than ever, altering how they approach insurance. People now seek clarity and transparency in policies, actively researching options before making decisions. They prefer digital interactions, leaning towards online platforms for purchasing and managing their insurance. This trend is particularly prevalent among younger generations, who value convenience and speed.

Additionally, there is a growing desire for flexibility in insurance products; consumers favor options that allow them to adjust coverage as their life circumstances change, such as starting a family or buying a home. This shift is pushing insurers to create more adaptable policies with customizable features. Furthermore, consumers are increasingly concerned about value for money, rejecting one-size-fits-all solutions and looking for products that offer real benefits tailored to their specific needs. Insurers recognize this demand and strive to develop products that resonate with consumers' values and lifestyles, ensuring they remain relevant in a competitive market.

The Role of Technology in Policy Management

The insurance industry has seen significant changes in recent years, largely due to InsurTech innovations that have transformed how policies are applied for and managed. Traditional methods often involved lengthy paperwork, convoluted processes, and frustrating communications. Today, technology simplifies these tasks, making the entire experience smoother for consumers. With processes now streamlined through online platforms and mobile apps, applying for insurance can feel almost effortless. Many companies offer instant quotes, allowing potential policyholders to compare options quickly and conveniently.

Moreover, digital tools help in managing insurance policies more efficiently. Through secure apps, users can track their policies, make payments, and even file claims with just a few taps on their smartphones. You no longer need to wait on hold or search for paperwork; everything is conveniently housed within a single platform. This enhanced accessibility means that families can focus more on their financial planning and less on administrative tasks, making their insurance coverage a proactive part of their wealth-building strategies.

Managing life insurance can be manageable, especially with various digital tools. Many apps designed for insurance management allow users to store policy documents safely. This eliminates the hassle of physical paperwork, enabling quick access whenever required. Some apps offer helpful reminders for premium payments or policy renewals, ensuring you get all crucial deadlines. There's also the added benefit of receiving notifications about changes in policy benefits or rates, which can impact your financial planning.

Diving deeper, these digital platforms often provide educational resources to guide you through understanding your policy types and options for maximizing your potential benefits. By keeping your insurance information organized and easily accessible, you take a crucial step toward integrating life insurance into your overall financial strategy. Leveraging technology simplifies management and enhances your ability to make informed decisions about your family's financial future. Regularly engaging with these tools can help you stay on top of your insurance needs, ensuring you're always prepared for what lies ahead.

Emerging Products and New Market Opportunities

Innovative life insurance products are reshaping the market, providing versatile options that cater to diverse needs. One noteworthy trend is the emergence of hybrid policies that combine life insurance with long-term care benefits. These products aim to cover the financial implications of untimely death and the potential costs associated with aging and health care needs. Such policies address the growing concern over managing long-term care expenses, making them attractive for younger families planning for the future.

Additionally, the introduction of index universal life insurance has gained traction. These policies allow policyholders to benefit from market growth while providing a safety net against market downturns. The interest credited to these policies is often tied to a stock market index, offering a balance between risk and reward. This structure makes them appealing to those seeking security and growth potential. As technology advances, digital-first insurance offerings are also on the rise, allowing consumers to easily manage coverage through mobile apps, enhancing accessibility and convenience.

Spotting new opportunities in the insurance landscape requires vigilance and a keen understanding of market trends. One practical approach is to stay informed about regulatory changes, which often create new niches that can be leveraged. For example, recent shifts in tax policy or consumer protection laws may open doors for new product offerings or investment strategies. By attending industry conferences, participating in webinars, and engaging with thought leaders, individuals can gain insights highlighting under-served market segments or emerging demands.

Another method to identify opportunities is to conduct thorough market research. Analyzing demographic shifts, such as the growth of millennials entering the home-buying market, can reveal a demand for affordable life insurance products tailored to this group. The key lies in understanding the specific needs of your target audience, such as flexibility or investment options. Engaging with clients through surveys or feedback sessions can help unravel what features they find most valuable, guiding the development of products that resonate.

Remember that successful insurance strategies are about more than just coverage; they are linked to educating clients about their choices. The more informed consumers are, the better they will recognize the potential benefits of modern life insurance products. Providing clear, straightforward information on how these products can serve as wealth-building tools will enhance customer satisfaction and create a loyal client base ready to explore new offerings.

14. How to Choose Your Insurance Provider

Evaluating Financial Stability and Ratings

Evaluating an insurance provider's financial stability begins with understanding its ratings. Insurance ratings are assessments conducted by independent agencies that evaluate an insurer's financial strength. These ratings consider various factors, including the provider's financial history, management, market position, and claims-paying abilities. By learning how to interpret these ratings, consumers can make informed choices about which insurers will likely be there when they need them the most.

When analyzing insurance ratings, it's essential to look for agencies with a strong reputation, such as A.M. Best, Standard & Poor's, or Moody's. Each agency uses different criteria, but generally, a higher rating indicates a more financially stable company. Look for insurers with ratings in the A range or above, as these are more likely to meet their obligations and handle claims efficiently. Additionally, trends in ratings can provide insight into whether a company is improving or declining.

Researching the performance of various insurance carriers involves utilizing multiple resources to gather the necessary data. Start with online tools and comparison websites that aggregate information about various insurance companies, allowing you to review their ratings and claim settlement ratios. These platforms can help you see how different companies stack up against each other in terms of financial health and customer satisfaction.

You can delve deeper by reading reports from regulatory bodies and insurance commissions, which often publish data on complaints and customer feedback. This information can be incredibly valuable for understanding how a company handles claims and serves its customers over time. Talking to financial advisors or insurance agents can also provide personalized insights into which carriers may best suit your needs. Remember, thorough research not only builds your confidence in your choice of carrier but also ensures that you and your family are protected by a stable provider with a proven track record.

It is wise to remember that financial stability is not just about the numbers; it also reflects how a company treats its policyholders. Be sure to consider customer service ratings and testimonials for your overall evaluation. Evaluating all these aspects can help you select an insurance provider to safeguard your family's future.

Importance of Customer Service and Reviews

Strong customer service plays a crucial role in your insurance experience. When dealing with life insurance, having a responsive, knowledgeable, and empathetic customer service team makes all the difference. Insurance can often be a complicated topic, and you'll likely have many questions. Whether you need assistance with understanding policy details, filing a claim, or learning about your coverage options, it's essential to have access to representatives who are willing to invest time to help you navigate these challenges. A company that prioritizes customer service will not only help ensure that you feel supported, but it can also significantly impact your overall satisfaction with the service provided. Knowing someone is there for you during difficult times can provide a sense of security that enhances your relationship with your insurance provider.

Online reviews are an invaluable resource for choosing the right insurance provider. They offer real-life perspectives from individuals who have already had experiences with the company you are considering. By leveraging customer feedback, you can gain insights into how a company handles issues and how they treat their clients overall. Pay attention to review patterns, as they can reveal consistent strengths or weaknesses in the customer service experience. Positive reviews may highlight quick claims processing and helpful customer support, while negative reviews might indicate delays and poor communication. Understanding these aspects can empower you to make informed decisions, guiding you toward providers who align with your expectations and priorities.

Understanding Policy Terms and Carrier Options

Decoding policy language can feel like learning a new language entirely. Many life insurance policies come with complex, intimidating terms, but understanding them is essential for making informed decisions. Start with the basics: terms like premium, which refers to the amount you pay for your coverage, or deductible, the amount you'll need to pay out-of-pocket before your insurance kicks in. Knowing what a beneficiary is can also be crucial; this is the person or entity that will receive the policy benefits upon your passing. Other common terms include coverage limit, the maximum amount the insurer will pay out, and cash value, associated with permanent life policies, where part of your premium goes towards building a savings component. Familiarizing yourself with these and other key terms will empower you to navigate your policy confidently and ensure you choose the right coverage for your needs.

When comparing carrier options, you need to evaluate which insurance company aligns best with your financial goals. Not all insurers are created equal, and factors like customer service, financial stability, and policy types offered can make a significant difference in your experience. Start by looking into the insurer's ratings, which reflect their ability to pay claims. Company reviews and customer feedback are also valuable when assessing an insurance carrier. Consider how flexible each carrier is regarding policy options and whether they provide add-ons that could enhance your coverage. An often-overlooked aspect is the insurer's claims process; it's important to know how straightforward it is to file a claim and whether their customer service is helpful during such times. Ultimately, aligning your choice of insurance carrier with your long-term financial objectives means selecting a company you can trust to be there for you and your loved ones when it matters most.

Understanding policy terms and evaluating carrier options are integral steps in protecting your future. Ensuring that you have a firm grasp of the language surrounding life insurance boosts your confidence and enhances your ability to advocate for yourself and your family. When comparing carriers, prioritize those that meet your coverage needs and resonate with your financial aspirations. Being thorough in these areas will significantly contribute to crafting a solid financial strategy that covers your family and supports your wealth-building efforts.

15. Becoming a DIY Financial Planner

Resources for Self-Education on Insurance

A wealth of books and online courses are available for those looking to understand life insurance better. These resources guide readers through the fundamentals of life insurance, helping them grasp how it works and fits into broader financial planning. Graduates of these courses often praise comprehensive titles like The Insurance Bible, which delves into different types of insurance policies and their specific benefits. Platforms like Udemy and Coursera offer specialized online courses taught by industry experts, covering everything from policy selection to risk management. These courses often include interactive elements such as quizzes and discussion forums, making learning more engaging. Whether you choose a traditional book or a digital course, these resources empower individuals to assess their insurance needs effectively and make informed decisions, ensuring a solid foundation for financial security.

In addition to books and courses, attending webinars and workshops can further deepen one's understanding of insurance strategies. These live sessions, often hosted by financial advisors or insurance professionals, provide insights into the industry's latest trends and best practices. Webinars typically cover contemporary topics like leveraging life insurance for retirement planning or discussing changes in tax regulations that impact insurance products. On the other hand, workshops often provide hands-on experiences where participants can engage in case studies or simulations, allowing them to apply what they've learned in real-world scenarios. These interactive learning opportunities can enhance financial literacy and confidence in making insurance-related decisions. Engaging with these resources can open up new avenues for wealth building, ensuring participants are well-prepared to secure their financial future.

As you explore these resources, consider setting specific learning goals to measure your progress. This approach can help maintain motivation and clarity in understanding how life insurance can serve your broader financial objectives.

Tools to Analyze and Compare Insurance Policies

Understanding life insurance can feel overwhelming, especially with many policies available. Fortunately, financial comparison tools have become vital resources to simplify this process. These tools allow you to compare various life insurance options, highlighting key features, costs, and benefits. Many online platforms provide calculators, enabling users to estimate premiums based on personal information such as age, health status, and coverage needs. Some tools even present personalized recommendations based on your financial objectives and family situation, ensuring you have the information to make informed choices. By entering your preferences and needs, these tools help you sift through available policies, making it easier to find the ones that align with your goals, whether you are primarily focused on affordability, features, or long-term benefits.

Creating a comparison chart can be invaluable in evaluating different life insurance policies. Start by outlining the specific features that matter most to you, such as premium costs, death benefits, policy types, riders, and other relevant aspects. Using a simple spreadsheet can make this process easier. In your chart, list the names of the insurance companies in the first column and the features you want to compare across the top row. As you research, fill in the corresponding cells with details about each policy. This visual representation lets you see how the options stack up against one another at a glance. Please pay special attention to policy limitations and exclusions, as these can definitely affect your decision. By organizing information in this way, it becomes clearer which policy offers the best balance of coverage and cost, ultimately guiding you toward a choice that secures your family's future financially. A practical approach is periodically revisiting this chart as your needs and market options change.

A simple yet powerful tip is to incorporate any personal modifications or notes directly into your comparison chart. This will help you remember the nuances of each policy and any particular concerns you may have. This approach not only aids in choosing the right policy but also builds confidence in discussing options with insurance agents.

Building a Comprehensive Financial Plan, Including Insurance

Life insurance plays a vital role in integrated financial planning. Aligning your life insurance policies with your overall financial goals is essential. Start by assessing your current financial situation, including income, expenses, and savings. Understanding your financial landscape allows you to identify how much coverage you need and which type of policy fits your plan. For instance, term life insurance typically offers high coverage at a lower cost, making it suitable for young families who need protection while raising children. Whole life or universal life policies can be integrated into retirement planning, as they provide a death benefit and accumulate cash value over time. This cash value can be accessed through loans or withdrawals, adding another layer of financial flexibility when needed.

Reviewing your life insurance needs regularly is crucial, especially as life events occur, such as the birth of a child, purchasing a home, or advancing in your career. Each of these milestones can significantly impact your financial obligations and goals. Collaborating with a financial advisor can help you navigate these changes effectively, ensuring that your life insurance policy aligns with your broader financial strategy. Regularly updating your beneficiaries and policy details also ensures that your family is well-protected and that your investments are growing consistent with your overall wealth-building objectives.

Aligning your insurance choices with long-term financial goals requires a thoughtful approach to protection and wealth-building. When considering your long-term strategies, start by defining your financial objectives, such as saving for retirement, funding a child's education, or creating a legacy. These goals can influence the type of life insurance best suited for you. For example, cash-value life insurance policies can serve dual purposes: providing necessary life coverage while acting as a long-term savings vehicle. This strategy can be especially effective for those looking to build wealth over decades.

Life insurance, as part of your wealth strategy, can offer significant tax advantages, as the death benefit remains tax-free for your beneficiaries. Additionally, the growth in the cash value of permanent insurance typically accumulates on a tax-deferred basis, which can help maximize your savings. As you plan your retirement, consider how your insurance policies can complement your income sources. This synergy can provide both financial security and access to funds that can be used for unexpected expenses in retirement. By regularly reviewing your long-term goals and insurance portfolio, you can ensure that your policies evolve to meet your changing needs, ultimately supporting your quest for financial security and wealth accumulation.

Always consult with professionals who can provide tailored advice based on your unique situation and goals. This proactive approach ensures that your life insurance is more than just a safety net; it can be a powerful tool in your financial planning arsenal.

Conclusion

Your Next Steps Toward a Secure and Prosperous Future

First, I want to congratulate you on making it this far. You've taken a huge step toward understanding how life insurance can be more than just a safety net—it can be a cornerstone for building wealth and securing your future.

But as we both know, knowledge without action is like having a map and never taking the journey. Now that you've equipped yourself with the insights and strategies in this book, it's time to put them to work for you and your loved ones.

Ready to Take Control of Your Financial Future?

The journey doesn't stop here. If you're ready to take the next step—whether you need guidance on applying these strategies, exploring your life insurance options, or getting personalized advice tailored to your unique situation—I'm here to help.

Let's Connect

Visit my website, iamsevy.com, where you'll find:

- **Exclusive resources** to complement what you've learned in this book

- **Blog posts** with ongoing tips and insights to keep you informed

- **Links to my social media** for daily wisdom on wealth-building and financial security

- **A scheduler** for one-on-one consultations so we can tackle your personal financial goals together

Book a Consultation Today

During our consultation, we'll sit down (virtually or in person) to:

- Assess your current financial situation and goals

- Identify the life insurance strategies that work best for you

- Map out a personalized plan that not only secures your future but helps build wealth for generations to come

- Answer any questions you may have about making life insurance work for you

Don't let this book be the end of your journey—let it be the beginning of something much greater. Together, we can turn what you've learned here into a plan that brings financial peace of mind and prosperity to you and your family.

Visit iamsevy.com today and take that first step toward a future where your financial goals are within reach and your legacy is secure.

Remember, your future is too important to leave to chance. Let's work together to make your wealth-building goals a reality.

I look forward to helping you take control and build the secure future you deserve.

Warm regards,

Severen Henderson

Author of *Securing Your Future: The Smart Guide to Life Insurance and Wealth Building*

www.ingramcontent.com/pod-product-compliance
Lightning Source LLC
Chambersburg PA
CBHW070418230526
45471CB00006B/2866